W I L D C A T S !

O F   N O R T H   A M E R I C A

COUGAR

By Jalma Barrett
Photographs by Larry Allan

BLACKBIRCH PRESS, INC.

WOODBRIDGE, CONNECTICUT

Published by Blackbirch Press, Inc.
260 Amity Road
Woodbridge, CT 06525

Email: staff@blackbirch.com
Web site: www.blackbirch.com

Dedication
For Brian

–JB and LA

Printed in the United States

10 9 8 7 6 5 4 3 2 1

Photo Credits
Page 17: Bob and Clara Calhoun/Bruce Coleman Inc.; page 18 (top and bottom): ©E & P Bauer/Bruce Coleman Inc.; page 19: ©Tom Brakefield/Bruce Coleman Inc.; page 21: ©Bruce Coleman Inc.

Library of Congress Cataloging-in-Publication Data
Barrett, Jalma.
Cougar / text by Jalma Barrett : photographs by Larry Allan. — 1st ed.
    p.   cm. — (Wildcats of North America)
  Includes bibliographical references (p. 24) and index.
  Summary: Describes the cougar and its natural habitat, including physical traits, social life, survival instincts, birth and development, and interaction with humans.
  ISBN 1-56711-258-7 (lib. bdg. : alk. paper)
  1. Pumas—Juvenile literature. [1. Pumas.] I. Allan, Larry, ill. II. Title. III. Series: Barrett, Jalma. Wildcats of North America.
QL737.C23B2655   1999
599.75'24—dc21
          98-9876
          CIP
          AC

Contents

Introduction—Cougar: Our Biggest Cat

They're actually called by four different names: *Puma, Panther, Mountain Lion, Cougar.* No matter what they're called, they're the same magnificent animal. The oldest of these names is *puma*, which is the name given by the Inca Indians of South America. There are probably more than 50,000 cougars living in North America today. The cougar is the most wide-ranging wildcat in all the Americas. Cougars live in Canada, the U.S., Mexico, Central America, and South America. They can even be found all the way at the extreme southern area of Argentina, a place called Patagonia. Nowhere in the world does any other mammal, except humans, have such a huge north–south range.

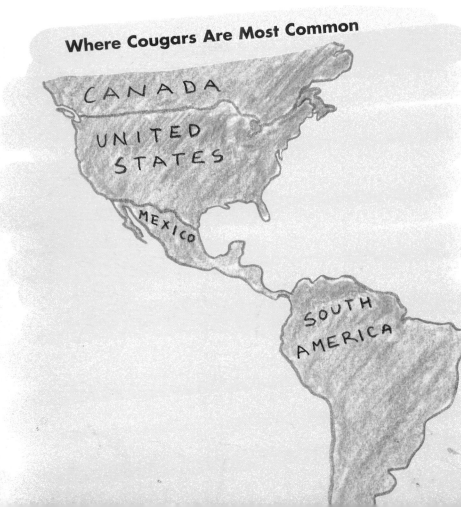

Where Cougars Are Most Common

CANADA

UNITED STATES

MEXICO

SOUTH AMERICA

Cougars are
also called
mountian lions,
panthers, and
pumas.

5

The Cougar's Environment

As the name *mountain lion* suggests, cougars generally live in mountainous areas. But they are also comfortable living in semi-arid (dry) regions and tropical forests. Some, like the Florida panther, even live in swamps. In North America, cougars are found mostly in western areas: British Columbia and Alberta in Canada; Oregon, California, Colorado, New Mexico, Montana, Wyoming, Washington, and west Texas in the United States. They also live throughout Mexico. Cougars might *migrate* (move seasonally) down from their mountain homes in winter to follow deer and other prey.

Name That Cat

A small zoo in Arizona prepared a cougar for shipment by air to another zoo across the country. After they carefully installed their cougar in its crate, they identified the contents of the crate as a "Cougar." The airline rejected the shipment. They said, "We don't accept cougars or mountain lions for shipment. It's standard airline policy. Too dangerous!"

After thinking about this problem, the zoo people changed the label on the cougar's crate. The second time around the airline accepted the animal without any comment. The new sign read, "P-u-m-a." 🐾

Rocky landscapes are excellent homes for cougars.

The Cougar Body

The cougar's physical features vary from one habitat to another. For instance, the Florida panther weighs between 75 and 80 pounds (34 to 36 kilograms). Cougars in Canada, however, have been known to weigh up to 275 pounds (125 kilograms)!

Cougars appear to have small heads. Really, they just look small on their big, powerful bodies. They have very long tails. Their tails can grow from 21 inches (53 centimeters) to more than 3 feet (1 meter) long, with a dark tip. Their ears are short and rounded, and dark on the back. Adult cougars are a tawny (golden tan) color, with dark markings on their heads. Cougars have long, strong legs. They also have big feet. Even though they are large, cougars are graceful animals.

Left: Cougars are known for their large paws and black-tipped tails.
Opposite: When a cougar runs, its front and back feet come down very close together.

The footprints, or tracks, of a cougar are quite round. Their four lower toes show in their tracks, but not the claws. Their claws are usually *retracted*, or drawn in, as they travel. The print of their front foot is about 4 inches (10 centimeters) long; the hindfoot's print is slightly smaller. When a cougar is *bounding* (running fast in leaps), its front and back feet come down very close together. In snow, their prints appear somewhat larger, and sometimes—especially in deep snow—their tails leave a slight drag mark between their paw prints.

Social Life

Cougars mostly live alone. Sometimes the territories of a male and a female cougar will overlap a bit. The males spend a lot of time marking the boundaries of their territories. They make their markings with *scrapes*, a pile of dirt kicked up by their hindfeet. Sometimes they'll create a loose pile of leaves or other material and urinate on it to create a territorial scent mark. Cougars also leave their marks by scratching on trees. Their scratch marks are fairly high up, and the marks are rather long. A cougar will also leave *feces* (droppings) as a scent mark. Sometimes it is uncovered, other times it is partly covered. If it has been covered, the scratching marks on the ground will indicate which direction the cougar was traveling. Cats always face in their direction of travel as they scratch.

A cougar will—like all other cats—groom itself. Usually, the grooming is done in a specific order. A cougar will start by licking its favorite front paw and using that paw like a washcloth on its face and behind its ears.

Cougars will spend a lot of time marking the trees and ground of their territory.

Then it will do the other front paw, washing the opposite side. Next, it will lick each shoulder and each front leg. Its sides are next to be groomed, then its back legs. The tail is done last. Pet house cats follow this same washing routine. On a hot day, evaporation of the wet saliva on its fur cools down a cougar's whole body.

Expert Hunters

Cougars hunt by *stalking* and *ambushing* their prey. This means they hide and attack by surprise. Cougars hunt most often on the ground. But they will also hunt from high rocks, low cliffs, or trees. Cougars are excellent jumpers and good climbers. They're able to leap 30 feet (9 meters) in a single bound. And they can jump 18 feet (5.5 meters) up into the branches of a tree. They move through trees quickly and with great ease. Cougars can drop 65 feet (20 meters) to the ground without injury.

A cat will shift its weight onto its back legs before leaping forward.

Sometimes a cougar will wait for prey to pass by to ambush it. A cougar will move forward slowly and silently, following its prey. Its belly will almost touch the ground, as it gets ready to leap. A cougar will try to stalk within 30 feet (9 meters) of its prey. When a cougar gets close enough, it will rush its victim. Cougars can run almost silently, partly because they have thick fur padding on their feet.

While stalking, a wild-cat will make itself low to the ground.

It will keep its hindlegs on the ground for support and stability as it leaps on the prey's back. Then it will bite it in the back of the neck. Some cougars have been known to kill a bear or bison with a single bite this way.

13

White-tailed deer are a cougar's favorite food, and cougars can outrun deer for short distances. Cougars will also eat beavers, coyotes, sheep, goats, porcupines, raccoons, peccaries (wild pigs), mice, rabbits and hares, birds, and even grasshoppers.

A cougar might kill one deer per week in areas where deer are plentiful. A deer is more food than a single cougar can eat at one time. To save the leftovers, a cougar will loosely cover the deer's remains with leaves and sticks.

Stalking prey through the snow

Then he will come back to eat more another day. This saved food is called a *cache*. The cougar might return to its cache several times over a period of days.

Cougars actually play an important role in the natural food web. They help to keep it in proper balance. For example, they help to keep the deer population from growing too large. This way, the deer's habitat can support the herd with enough food.

Dusk and dawn are the favorite hunting times for cougars. In quiet areas, far away from people, a cougar might hunt during the day. When people are nearby, cougars hunt only at night to avoid contact with humans. A male cougar can travel 25 miles (40 kilometers) in one night as it hunts for food. Because a cougar's sense of smell isn't too good, it generally locates prey by sight or sound.

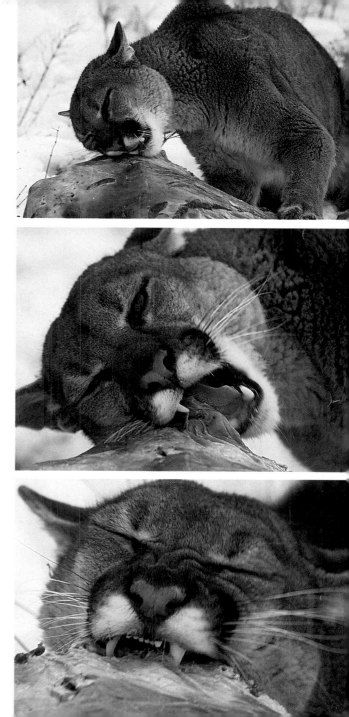

Top, middle, bottom: This cougar feasts on an elk that was killed by an avalanche.

The Mating Game

Cougars only pair up when it's time to mate. At that point, they'll spend about 2 weeks hunting and sleeping together. Then they go their separate ways. Males are sexually mature at about 2 years. They are capable of breeding until they're at least 20. Females mature at about 3 years, and can get pregnant until age 12. Females mate once every 2 years. Cougars have no fixed or specific mating season, like other wildcats do.

The "yowl" sound a cougar makes when it's seeking a mate is often compared to the sound of a woman crying loudly. Cougars can also growl or hiss when they're angry.

Like housecats, bobcats, and lynx, cougars can purr. These animals have solid *hyoid bones* at the base of their tongues. These bones are "U" shaped. When air is pushed up through the bone, it vibrates in a "purr" sound. Purring is a sign of relaxation and happiness. Cougars, however, cannot roar. Lions, tigers, and leopards—who can roar—have a band of flexible bone (cartilage) on their hyoid bones. This allows them to roar, but it prevents them from continuously purring. Lions, tigers, and leopards can only purr when they exhale.

Males and females will stay together for about 2 weeks during their mating period.

Cubs

Cougars have litters of 1 to 6 cubs. They are usually born in midsummer, 82 to 98 days after mating. The males do not help raise the young. Cubs are born blind and weigh about 14 ounces (397 grams) at birth—the size of a 6-week-old pet kitten. Cubs are born in a maternity den, which is a protected cave or shelter lined with moss and other plants. Cougar cubs are light yellow, with black spots and rings on their tails. There are no spots on cougars after they reach about 6 months of age.

A few weeks after birth, the cubs begin to explore—with mother watching closely. Cubs are *weaned* at about 3 months. That means they are no longer allowed to breastfeed. They don't go hungry, though.

By the time they are 6 weeks old, cougar cubs are eating meat and exploring on their own.

Since they were 6 weeks old, their mother has been bringing them meat. At 3 months, the cubs begin to hunt with their mother.

Cougars communicate with each other by licking, rubbing each other, and vocalizing. Cougar mothers whistle like birds at their cubs—sometimes softly, sometimes loudly enough to almost hurt eardrums! The young often respond with loud, chirping whistles of their own. Cubs also mew, like a house cat does.

Climbing trees and playing with other cubs teaches young cougars the skills they will use in hunting.

19

Florida Panther: Endangered Species!

At one time, the Florida panther ranged from the lower Mississippi River area eastward to Florida and the Atlantic coast. Today, there are only 40 to 50 adult Florida panthers living in the wild.

The Florida panther, the smallest cougar, is quickly nearing *extinction*. This means they are dying out. The reason they have nearly disappeared is because their habitat has been so severely reduced by humans.

An adult male panther needs a territory of between 200 and 300 square miles (518 to 777 square kilometers) in order to get enough food to eat. It needs to be in a secluded (hidden) habitat, where there is little or no possible contact with humans. People have moved into Florida in such numbers that most of the panther's habitat has been turned into areas of homes, businesses, and other places for human activity.

The U.S. Fish and Wildlife Service, the National Park Service, the Florida Game and Fresh Water Fish Commission, and the Florida Department of Environmental Protection have banded together to create a recovery program. To learn more about these private cats, they are placing radio collars on Florida panthers. To strengthen breeding stock, they also introduced eight female Texas cougars to the region. These animals are the closest relative of the Florida panther. These Texas females have borne a number of kittens in Florida, which could signal a brighter future for these wonderful creatures.

Cougar cubs learn how to hunt with their play. As practice, cubs will *pounce* on (jump on and take hold of) their mother's waving tail. Or, they'll pounce on a leaf. Sometimes they will wait to ambush another cub from the litter. The mother cougar also bats around pieces of meat with her paws to encourage her youngsters to "hunt" before she allows them to eat. When they are older, cubs also watch their mother hunt. The mother patiently teaches by example, showing her young cubs how to correct their mistakes. This prepares them for adult life. It shows them how to stalk and attack prey.

By 3 to 4 months of age, cougar cubs have learned much about hunting from their mother.

Cougars and Humans

The cougar population of North America is declining. This decline is due mainly to hunting by the cougar's only predator: humans. Some of the decline may also be due to the disappearance in some areas of the cougar's main food source, the white-tailed deer. Wolves also prey on baby cougars. Cougars have occasionally been known to injure or kill people. But they tend to avoid contact with humans.

Cougars need to be left alone by humans in order to survive.

There were 9 attacks by cougars on humans in California between 1986 and 1996. This was probably because more people are moving into cougar territories. Only 3 attacks were recorded there in the 100 years before 1986. Hunters have been hired to kill cougars in some areas. These people mistakenly believe that cougars are a threat to livestock. Where natural game is abundant, cougars do not disturb domestic animals. Cougars are protected by law where their numbers are small. Unfortunately, where cougars are plentiful, this cat is classified as a "game animal" (allowed to be hunted).

Like all creatures on Earth, cougars need our protection and respect. If we allow them to live their lives peacefully, they will remain one of nature's most graceful and majestic creatures.

Feline Facts

Name: Cougar

Scientific Name: *Felis concolor*

Shoulder Height: 24" to 28" (61 to 71 cm)

Body Length: 51" to 71" (13 to 20 meters)

Tail Length: 21" to 37" (53 cm to 1 meter)

Weight: 75 to 275 pounds (36 to 125 kilograms)

Color: Tawny (golden tan), unspotted

Reaches sexual maturity: Females at 3 years; males at 2 years

Females mate: Once every 2 years

Gestation (pregnancy period): 82 to 98 days

Litter Size: 1 to 6 cubs (usual size is 2 to 3)

Social Life: Lives alone

Favorite Food: White-tail deer

Habitat: Mountains, but also semi-arid areas, subtropical and tropical forests, and swamps in western Canada, western U.S., Florida, and Mexico

Glossary

ambush To hide and then attack.
bounding Running in fast leaps.
cache A hidden supply.
extinct No longer in existence.
feces Bodily wastes; droppings.
hyoid bones U-shaped bones at the base of a tongue.
migrate Move from area to area based on the season and food source.

pounce To jump on and then take hold of something.
scrapes A pile of dirt kicked up by a cat's hindfeet.
stalking To hunt or track in a quiet, secret way; usually following prey.
weaned No longer breastfeeding.

Further Reading

Funston, Sylvia. *Eastern Cougar* (Endangered Animal series). San Diego, CA: Owl Communications, 1992.

Hodge, Deborah. *Wild Cats: Cougars, Bobcats and Lynx*. Ontario: Kids Can Press, 1997.

Perry, Phyllis J. *The Snow Cats* (First Books—Animals series). Danbury, CT: Franklin Watts, 1997.

Stone, Lynn M. *Cougars* (Early Bird Nature Books). Minneapolis, MN: Lerner Publications Company, 1997.

Index